POWER UP YOUR CLASSROOM

REIMAGINE LEARNING THROUGH GAMEPLAY

LINDSEY BLASS
AND CATE TOLNAI

International Society for Technology in Education
PORTLAND, OREGON ■ ARLINGTON, VIRGINIA

Power Up Your Classroom
Reimagine Learning through Gameplay
Lindsey Blass and Cate Tolnai

Editor: *Emily Reed*
Copy Editor: *Jennifer Weaver-Neist*
Proofreader: *Corinne Gould*
Indexer: *Wendy Allex*
Book Design and Production: *Mayfly Design*
Cover Design: *Edwin Ouellette*

Library of Congress Control Number: 2021933220

First Edition
ISBN: 978-1-56484-798-0
Ebook version available.

Printed in the United States of America
ISTE® is a registered trademark of the International Society for Technology in Education.

ABOUT ISTE

The International Society for Technology in Education (ISTE) is the premier nonprofit organization serving educators and education leaders committed to empowering connected learners in a connected world. ISTE serves more than 100,000 education stakeholders throughout the world.

ISTE's innovative offerings include the ISTE Conference & Expo, one of the biggest, most comprehensive edtech events in the world—as well as the widely adopted ISTE Standards for learning, teaching, and leading in the digital age and a robust suite of professional learning resources, including webinars, online courses, consulting services for schools and districts, books, and peer-reviewed journals and publications. Visit ISTE.org to learn more.

Related ISTE Titles

Gamify Literacy: Boost Comprehension, Collaboration and Learning, edited by Michele Haiken (2017)

To see all books available from ISTE, please visit **iste.org/resources**.

ABOUT THE AUTHORS

 **Lindsey Blass** is the personalized learning environments program manager for San Francisco Unified School District. Serving the largest, public, urban school district in the Bay Area, Lindsey develops systems and processes to leverage technology and learning-environment design to promote academic and socio-emotional growth for all students, with an emphasis in reaching historically underserved student populations. As adjunct faculty for Krause Center for Innovation at Foothill College (in Los Altos Hills, California) and a Google Certified Innovator, she is a leader in the field of educational technology. Lindsey is a sought-after speaker on the topics of gamification and game-based learning (GBL), and is the cofounder of #PlayPD, an "unconference" movement designed to leverage the power of gameplay to engage educators in designing innovative learning experiences. She believes that learning should be *fun* for both teachers and students, and strives to create dynamic and engaging learning experiences that inspire lifelong learners.

You can connect with Lindsey on her website, **LindseyBlass.com**, and through Twitter **@LindseyBlass1**.

 **Cate Tolnai** is the director of member engagement for California's ISTE affiliate CUE (Computer-Using Educators), an education nonprofit for innovation in learning and leading throughout California and Nevada. She is a passionate fan of learning, coaching, and connecting. In her fifteenth year in K–12 education, Cate serves educators as they integrate technology-rich, future-ready learning. She has spent ten years in K–12 classrooms and five years coaching teachers and administrators at both the district and county levels. As a Google Certified Innovator and Google for Education Certified Trainer and adjunct faculty for Krause Center for Innovation

(at Foothill College in Los Altos Hills, California), she commits to supporting the integration of technology and teaching across grade levels and content areas. Cate is the cofounder of #Sketch50, a movement to incorporate visual creativity into learning; #TeachersNeedIt, a social movement prioritizing the basic and extended needs of all educators in bringing excellent instruction into the classroom; and #ConnectedTL, a network for teacher leaders. She loves to talk gamification, microcertifications, blended and online learning, personalized professional development (PD), learning through play, and finding reasons to celebrate every victory step.

You can connect with Cate on her website, Teachers Need It (**TeachersNeedIt.com**), and through Twitter **@CateTolnai**.

Acknowledgments

There are so many people who helped us make this book a reality:

To our PLN, who proves again and again that we are #bettertogether and inspires us to reimagine learning. You "walk the walk and talk the talk" each day, and we witness the dynamic and engaging learning environments you build. You constantly push us to become better educators.

To our amazing families, who put up with insanely long workdays and support us through our passion projects, so we can play a role in making education better.

To all our students who love games and remind us that classroom learning is best when we remember to keep you at the center.

To all blossoming educators who continue to ask "What if… ?" in their quest to design instruction with students at the core.

You *all* are our inspiration.

CONTENTS

FOREWORD

Built in the late 12th or early 13th century, the outer wall of the Bayon temple in Angkor, Cambodia has a bas-relief showing two people playing a board game. The tour guide claimed it was a chessboard, but it's more likely another ancient game, the name of which has now been lost. Fortunately, other ancient games have not been lost. Senet is the oldest board game ever discovered, for example. It is a randomized race game traced back to Predynastic Egypt, dating it at around 3100 B.C. Archeologists found the game buried with several ancient Egyptians.

Humankind has played games for a long, long time—even educational games. During the American Civil War, soldiers played a game called American Kriegsspiel, which was originally created in 1812 to train Prussian military officers. Modern-day computer games teach students how to be entrepreneurs.

Games, gamification, and play are attracting a great deal of attention these days—and rightfully so. There is a growing body of research describing how the concept of play is key to the psychological well-being of children and how a lack of play is linked, in dramatic ways, to an increase in mental-health issues in the developed world. It has been said that depriving children of the opportunity to have self-guided play deprives them of opportunities to learn how to take control of their own lives, how to make their own decisions, and how to mitigate conflicts on their own.

Play and games are fundamental human activities. They should be both encouraged and nurtured. Yet repeatedly, the old argument comes to the forefront: "Show the evidence that game-based learning leads to positive learning outcomes." I sometimes counter with, "Show the evidence that lecture-based instruction leads to positive learning outcomes."

I wrote my book *The Gamification of Learning and Instruction: Game-Based Methods and Strategies for Training and Education* out of frustration. I wanted to show that there is solid research—a great deal of solid research—on the efficacy of games for learning. I wanted to show that there is evidence to support claims that games are a powerful tool for learning, for strengthening communication skills, and for motivating participation and engagement.

But if there is evidence, then why aren't there more games in the classroom?

Until now, an important piece has been missing: a practical, step-by-step, informed guidebook to bring the gameplay experience intelligently into the classroom. This is where Lindsey Blass and Cate Tolnai excel. In *Power Up Your Classroom*, they have taken the theories, research, and history of games and distilled the concepts and elements of gameplay into practical, impactful classroom experiences.

This clever book is framed—as it should be—as a game. Within its game framework, you'll meet gaming experts (or "Game Masters"), be challenged to add gameplay to your classroom, and be encouraged to think like a game designer. Even better, you have the wisdom of two experts who will playfully help you rise to the challenge and level up! When you do so, you will literally be carrying on a five-thousand-year-old tradition.

Karl M. Kapp
Author of *The Gamification of Learning and Instruction*
and coauthor of *Play to Learn*

INTRODUCTION

Welcome, reader! This book is designed as a game that explores different elements of game design and shares ideas for incorporating games into your teaching. In the levels (chapters) that follow, you will hear from experienced Game Masters, uncover a framework for game-based learning (GBL), complete challenges, and share your learning. We hope that you enjoy the journey. Before diving in, however, we wanted to share our personal stories of how we discovered the joy of games.

LINDSEY'S STORY

On October 17, 1989, the Loma Prieta earthquake struck northern California with a magnitude of 6.9 and an intensity rating of violent. As the earthquake hit, I had just settled into my predinner routine: a coveted one hour of video-game time. I was deeply engrossed in Super Mario Bros., traveling through World 5-1—just one level away from the warp zone that would take me to World 8 (home of the final boss battle)—when the world started shaking (the *real* world, not the virtual world). The chandelier above the stairs slammed against the ceiling, sending shards of glass flying in all directions. The television fell, causing me to jump back, nearly missing the attack of the fifty-pound beast. I could hear my mom yelling frantically from the bottom of the stairs: "Girls! Get down here *now*!"

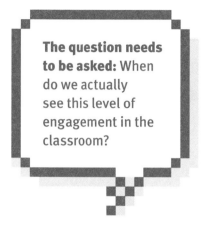

The question needs to be asked: When do we actually see this level of engagement in the classroom?

In the midst of this chaos, I made an interesting decision. With the comfort of my mother in one direction and the smashed TV in the other, I bolted back toward the television to grab the Nintendo controller and pause my game. This decision still comes back to me time and time again. What about this game made me so deeply immersed in the experience that I was willing to risk my physical safety in order to ensure my game wasn't interrupted?

As the years went by and I finished school (only to launch into a career as an educator), one truth became glaringly clear to me: Student engagement is a struggle. Many educators equate engagement with compliance, claiming that if students are on task and following along with the teacher's prescribed flow of a lesson, then they are "engaged."

I am reminded of the concept of "flow," conceived by psychologist Mihaly Csikszentmihalyi. According to Csikszentmihalyi, "Flow is the way people describe their state of mind when consciousness is harmoniously ordered, and they want to pursue whatever they are doing for its own sake." (2008) I believe real engagement is this experience of flow, where a student is so deeply immersed in a task that they will push forward despite all obstacles, even a violent earthquake. (*Side note*: I fully support earthquake safety and do not actually recommend students running back in the room to finish their lessons in the event of an earthquake.)

The question needs to be asked: when do we actually see this level of engagement in the classroom?

I believe that we can harness the power of play in education in order to create experiences that allow students to become deeply engaged agents and owners of their learning experience. I believe that as educators, we can design powerful learning experiences that spread our love of learning to the hearts and minds of our students.

CATE'S STORY

On August 31, 1980, I was born into the Samson family in Long Beach, California, as child number thirteen, girl number seven. To say my siblings were (and still are!) competitive is a gross understatement. Contests, races, and tournaments were regular pastimes in our house. Upon the news of my arrival into the world, my sisters whooped with joy—the girl's team won! Starting on day one of my life, I was on the winning team, and it felt awesome.

From basketball to volleyball to Pogs to jigsaw puzzles, I fell in love with the chase that each game brought. Whether I walked away a winner or a loser, each adventure gave me a chance to try something new and learn more about myself as a player.

Fast-forward 23 years. With blind confidence and a sparkle of hope in my eye, I entered my first classroom in Hell's Kitchen, New York City as a teacher ready to offer my ninth graders a new, fun-infused way of learning. I desperately wanted them to feel the same joy I felt when I took on a challenge and succeeded. While I may have entered the classroom that day with plenty of sympathy for my students, I had very little empathy for the realities they brought into our learning space. Over time and through many emotional challenges, I was humbled and changed.

When I returned home in 2004 to teach middle school in the Mid-City neighborhood of Los Angeles, I knew more about the unique makeup of urban classroom culture. No one wanted a gimmick; they could smell anything forced or fake from a mile away. So I took my passion for play and my love of learning to the next level. The game was on!

I designed my humanities classroom to be standards-aligned and experience-rich. Students explored virtual neolithic caves on the underside of folding tables. Our walls transformed into a Renaissance workshop, and my sixth graders worked alongside an imaginary Leonardo da Vinci as they learned to sketch and create. Using sound bites and vivid images, we sailed down the Nile River, exploring the fertile green valley surrounding our felucca and designing comic strips that documented our experience. Learning shifted from talking to doing and occurred from all angles in our space.

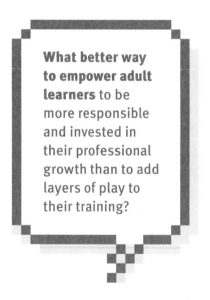

What better way to empower adult learners to be more responsible and invested in their professional growth than to add layers of play to their training?

Even so, a thought was heavy on my mind whenever I challenged my learners to play. Many of them feared criticism from their peers, and others didn't have the endurance to persevere when the challenge got steep. I wondered, "How can my students grow with more confidence and curiosity in the classroom?" It wasn't through traditional tests, essays, or worksheets; they needed to engage learning with emotions and feel connected to the concepts. How would they get there?

Play. Learning *must* be playful. If we hook our students and heighten the emotional connections to daily routines, we have a much better chance of competing with the increased stimuli of life in a digital world outside of school. I committed then and there to create a vibrant and memorable learning space that prioritized the hearts and minds of all my learners.

Since leaving the classroom and focusing primarily on professional learning leadership, I continue this commitment. If we want teachers to infuse their classrooms with energy and passion, we have to model this goal as professional learning leaders. Malcolm Knowles, founder of andragogy (adult learning theory), states: "Adults are self-directed and expect to take responsibility for decisions. Adult learning programs must accommodate this fundamental aspect." (2019)

What better way to empower adult learners to be more responsible and invested in their professional growth than to add layers of play to their training? I continue to see the joy and confidence of educators when they unbox a game and eventually design their own, and I believe those feelings trickle right into their classrooms and into the lives of their students.

OUR WHY

By the time our paths crossed, we each knew why we valued the power of educational gameplay. Both of us had traveled along a professional path from teacher to coach to central/county office roles focused on innovative learning design. As our friendship deepened, we noticed more and more similarities in our worlds. Regardless of location and socioeconomic status, our learners wanted and needed more personalized and meaningful instruction. We saw a few trends in our experiences:

> **Trend 1:** Learners who struggle to own and connect to their learning become disengaged.

> **Trend 2:** Both students and teachers experience fear of failure on a regular basis.

> **Trend 3:** Educators need support to design deeply engaging learning experiences and classroom environments where failure is celebrated as an opportunity for growth.

> **Trend 4:** Students coming from a failure-rich classroom experience regular choice and celebration, and show much higher levels of engagement in learning.

In her 2013 TEDx talk, "Living in Beta," Molly Bennett (formerly Schroeder) addresses the fear of failure we so often see in classrooms. She explains that our goal is to move students from point A to point B, yet point A looks different for each and every student. She suggests that we create classroom cultures similar to the culture of Google, where launching early and iterating often is part of the norm.

This concept of "living in beta" ties directly to gaming concepts that create a culture of confidence and risk-taking:

> **Multiple lives:** If your first chance was your only chance to master a game, you would never progress to mastery! How often is our first chance our only chance in learning?

> **Feedback:** If you had no clue how you were progressing in a game and what needed to be done to move on to the next level, would you still play? Of course not! How often do we build in feedback loops that allow our students to see their progress?

> **Meaning and higher purpose:** The small steps you take when playing a game lead to a higher achievement or goal. How often do students connect with a higher goal in their learning experience, or what gamification expert Yu-Kai Chou (**yukaichou.com**) calls "epic meaning and calling"?

So together, we began to wonder, "What if...?"

> **What if** educators experience the impact of gameplay firsthand and spread the excitement and innovation in their classrooms?

> **What if** educators leverage the power of gameplay to engage and motivate more learners?

> **What if** learning becomes *fun* for both students and teachers?

Figure 0.1. Responses to the question: What makes games fun?

OUR HOW

At the 2018 International Society for Technology in Education (ISTE) Conference & Expo, we asked our session participants, "What makes games fun?"

If you look closely at the words in **Figure 0.1**, you will notice that not one participant answered "reading the directions" (the gaming equivalent of reading the textbook). The top trending answers for what makes games fun were strategy, challenge, and competition. (Note: this does not always mean competition against peers and can involve competing against one's personal best.)

If these elements are enough to engage students into a state of flow, where they are fully and deeply immersed in the experience, how can they be leveraged to design more engaging learning experiences? In a 2018 study by Vanderbilt University, research showed that integration

Figure 0.2. #PowerUpClassroom Theory of Improvement for Education.

of curricula-aligned games led to significant increases in students' academic achievement, engagement in the learning experience, motivation, and critical thinking skills (Clark, Tanner-Smith, Hostetler, Fradkin, & Polikov, 2018).

Based on existing research and our personal experience, we propose a #PowerUpClassroom Theory of Improvement for Education (**Figure 0.2**). This theory identifies the work teachers can do to arrive at the highly desirable and attainable goal of engaged students who go on to be lifelong learners.

We have made it our mission to partner with educators to put game-based learning theory into action. This book provides extensive resources, research, real-world examples, and actionable input that empowers educators to design impactful learning experiences while leveraging the power of play.

Are you ready to transform your instruction?

Great! Let's power up your classroom!

FRAMING THE GAME: THE RULES

This book is designed as a quest that will help you power up learning experiences through game-based learning.

Throughout each level (chapter), you will discover tips, reflection points, and best practices of game-based learning in the form of "Power Up" sidebars. Consider the impact these golden nuggets have on game design, instructional design, and cultural shift in your learning space.

You'll be introduced to theory, pedagogy, and strategies around the effective integration of gameplay in the classroom and will hear from Game Masters (educators experienced in integrating gameplay into curricular design) on specific tools and strategies for implementation.

At the end of each level, you will unlock a challenge that moves you to the next level of the game. The skills you develop from completing these challenges will move you toward the larger goal of designing dynamic and engaging learning experiences. You may just become a Game Master yourself!

FRAMING THE GAME: THE JOURNEY

As you progress through the book and unlock the challenges in each level, watch your progress advance on the game board. Keep on moving and learning!

START

Define **#PowerUp Classroom Theory of Improvement for Education.**

Identify & explore the **#PowerUp Classroom 4 C's of GBL.**

Distinguish between **Gamification** and **GBL.**

Explore the power of play.

Empower students through choice.

Assess players' sources of motivation.

Explore the **#PowerUp Classroom GBL Design Framework.**

Clarify the role of technology in game design.

Value having fun with your learners.

Create an emotionally safe space.

Determine the purpose of student game design.

Apply **#PowerUp Classroom GBL Design Framework** to student games

Assess the impact of audience.

Establish the assessment potential of GBL.

Explain how GBL offers choice & clarification.

Assess mastery using GBL & gamification.

FINISH

Identify your next step with GBL!

Explore the power of celebration.

Assess your classroom cultural readiness.

Investigate the social-emotional dynamics of GBL.

LEVEL 1

BEYOND THE INSTRUCTION MANUAL: GOALS OF THE GAME

What gameplay structures already exist in learning, and how can the power of play increase learner engagement?

By the end of this level, you will be able to:

★ Identify the *#PowerUpClassroom 4 C's of Game-Based Learning (GBL)*
★ Make connections to how the *#PowerUpClassroom 4 C's of GBL* impact learning experiences for teachers and students
★ Identify the unique characteristics of gamification and game-based learning
★ Explore how the power of play can increase learner engagement

e invite you to journey into two worlds with us:

In the first world, students enter the classroom and take out their notebooks. The teacher presents the content for the day as the students take notes, asking clarifying questions as needed. The teacher models several problems for guided practice, and ultimately, the students apply their skills in independent practice and application.

In the second world, students are presented with a game-based challenge that requires research, collaboration, communication with peers, and creative problem-solving. They are able to power up as they progress, conquering the challenge only when they have mastered the content.

While both worlds contain elements of solid lesson design (i.e., input, guided practice, independent practice), in which world do you picture the students experiencing deeper engagement? Which world empowers students to reach mastery and experience success in learning?

By leveraging the power of play, we provide learners with purpose, motivation, and increased engagement in their learning experience.

 POWER UP

ENGAGEMENT AS A CLASSROOM CORNERSTONE

Every class or school community has a unique definition for the ideal engaged learner. That said, there are a few qualities that consistently connect to engagement: in-person or digital conversations, freedom to be curious and take risks socially and academically, and personal ownership of projects and outcomes. Remember, you can always ask your learners to define "engagement" for your classroom community.

MEET THE GAME MASTER

CATE TOLNAI, EDUCATOR AND ADVOCATE

GBL GROUND ZERO

One rainy afternoon in 2011, Cate's students quietly worked their way through the canned history curriculum lesson for another time, and she wondered, "How can we do better?" She wanted her students to *want* to take more risks, ask questions, and explore without fear of failure or punishment.

> *I believe that all learners are curious, and making space to explore that curiosity is our responsibility as educators.*

But how do we balance the pressure of getting through the content while also honoring learning for what it is: a journey, a quest, an exploration? As Cate moved into teacher-leadership roles, she quickly understood the reason why she was challenged to create these experiences for her students: no one had given *her* the chance to learn this way as a professional educator.

Cate sat through daylong workshops without ever being asked to work with the amazing educators around her. She attended staff meetings where she listened to administrators read agendas and slides without pause for reflection or discussion. She took notes, completed assignments, designed lessons, and evaluated curriculum—all without being fully engaged in the process. Something was missing.

EMBARKING ON THE JOURNEY

As a connected educator and curious learner, Cate began to design her vision for revitalized professional learning.

> *If we believe kids deserve the very best we can offer them via relationships, instructional materials, and tools, then how will we get that to them? It starts with excellent training for the educators leading the charge.*
>
> *Teachers need as many opportunities as possible to choose paths of learning, clarify skills and passions, connect with each other, and celebrate growth with their students.*
>
> *By creating high-quality professional learning that unpacks the resources we want to bring to our students, we build empathy in educators as well as a frame of reference to fall back on when they enter their classroom.*

The more Cate integrated play into professional training by creating both gamified and game-based learning opportunities, the more she saw these lessons trickle into classroom spaces. From classroom teachers to aspiring administrators to district and county staff members—we *all* need the time and space to unearth our inner gamer.

> *If we want to disrupt student learning, we must disrupt professional training for educators starting with the #PowerUpClassroom 4 C's of Game-Based Learning.*

#POWERUPCLASSROOM 4 C'S OF GBL

1. Choose: Learners experience choice in process and product

2. Clarify: Learners reflect on their progress in an iterative growth process

3. Connect: Learners build relationships through common progress, skills, interest, and goals

4. Celebrate: Learners have opportunities to celebrate both process and mastery of learning

 POWER UP

MODEL THE 4 C'S OF GBL EVERY DAY

Look for frequent opportunities to clarify the skills your learners are gaining and celebrate their growth in the community. Sometimes, a leaderboard sets a tone of accomplishment; other times, a mentor board is a better fit, going beyond the competition to connect your learners. Either way, find opportunities each day to shine light on your students (Transition Zone, 2018).

Cate's work with adult learners motivates her to create authentic and honest professional-learning experiences for educators.

Cate invites you to wonder:

> How can educators bring these experiences, this empathy, and this new expertise to their classrooms?
> How might professional learning truly reflect the best practices of classroom learning?

Access Cate's resources and passion projects at **www.catetolnai.com** and connect with her on Twitter **@CateTolnai**.

This book takes you on a quest to design dynamic and engaging learning experiences through gameplay. Your first task is to explore different instructional models that harness the power of play.

Let's start with the basic concepts. Quite often the terms "gamification" and "game-based learning" are used interchangeably, when in reality, they are two unique concepts, with different characteristics and features. Synthesizing the content from multiple books, studies, and lectures on these concepts, the following are basic breakdowns of widely agreed-upon definitions for the terms:

GAMIFICATION VERSUS GAME-BASED LEARNING

Gamification Defined

Applying the elements of game design in a non-game setting, such as instruction and training. The learning experience is supported by adding in elements typically associated with games.

Game-Based Learning (GBL) Defined

Learning occurs through gameplay. The game itself is the learning experience, and by playing the game, students reach the instructional objectives.

 POWER UP

KNOW YOUR TERMS

Based on the definitions we explored, gamification occurs when you apply game elements to traditional instruction. When learners engage in actual gameplay as the learning, they experience game-based learning. Keeping these terms straight helps keep you connected to your overall learning goal(s).

GAMIFICATION VERSUS GBL IN ACTION

Gamification in Action	Game-Based Learning in Action
A gamified classroom might set up quests that students embark on in order to reach an end goal. This leads to increased motivation toward the goal.	In game-based learning, curricular content is presented by playing a game.

Gamification in Action

Examples of this include:

➤ Badges to acknowledge accomplishments
➤ Point systems (either individual or competitive)
➤ Leaderboards to harness social motivation

Game-Based Learning in Action

Examples of this include:

➤ Educational board games
➤ Whole class games, such as Jeopardy
➤ Immersive digital experiences, such as learning math concepts by playing Minecraft

So why are these two terms so often confused? Perhaps it's the way they sound alike. Aside from their semantic similarity and the fact that they both focus on the power of play in learning, they can often go hand in hand.

Let's take a closer look at examples from Game Master Jacob Aringo's STEAM classroom.

MEET THE GAME MASTER

JACOB ARINGO, STEAM TEACHER

GAMIFICATION IN ACTION

Students in Jacob's gamified STEAM class don't just come to class, they join in for an adventure. Each course he teaches is framed through quests the students need to accomplish. Each quest contains missions, and at the end of every quest, there is a boss battle (a final battle to advance to the next quest.).

The adventure (or course) launches with a video that frames the journey the class will take during their learning experience. (Scan the QR code or visit **bit.ly/STEAMlaunch** to visit Jacob's course-launch video, which contains a challenge to his students to engineer their world with their ideas.)

Much of Jacob's work in gamifying his classroom is based on the theory and framework design of Yu-Kai Chou (**YuKaiChou.com**). Yu-Kai Chou advocates for moving beyond design that is only focused on integrating gamified elements (points, badges, and leaderboards) and focusing on core motivational drives that lead to increased motivation, engagement, and eventually, empowerment. The way Jacob frames his courses is based on the core drive of "Epic Meaning and Calling" as he works with his students (who he deems "Jedi Innovators") to defeat "Darth Boredom:"

> *When learning has a deeper purpose beyond getting straight As, satisfying their parents, ranking themselves amongst their peers, and getting into the college of their choice, the learners are able to focus on what matters most . . . their passion, which eventually and potentially translates into their future."*

Moving beyond gamifying the structures of his course design, Jacob's students also engage in game-based learning, where their learning experience occurs through both engaging in and designing games. (Learn more about Jacob's approach to student-designed games in Level 4.)

GAME-BASED LEARNING IN ACTION

Each of the quests that Jacob's students engage in contain missions. These missions are the actual course content that the students will need to engage in. A mission contains a single objective (which equates to one academic objective) that includes the key skills needed to beat the boss at the end. Boss battles are sometimes digital assessments of skills but can also include physical design challenges.

Jacob invites you to question:

> ➤ How are you evolving in your practice?
> ➤ How is your evolution affecting how your students are learning?

Access Jacob's resources, blog, and ongoing story at TeamAringo.org and connect with him on Twitter **@teamaringo**.

During our journey together, we will explore examples of both game-based learning and gamification in action, and discover how the symbiotic relationship between these two instructional strategies allows us to truly harness the power of play as lesson designers.

YOUR CHALLENGE

Choose a challenge from below to share either on Twitter or here in this book. Or better yet, choose to do both!

> In your own words, describe the difference between gamification and game-based learning.

> Explore your "why" for embarking on this journey. What do you hope to accomplish in bringing the power of play into your learning experiences?

Post your response to Twitter using #PowerUpClassroom.

ISTE STANDARDS CONNECTION
Let's Connect Your Learning to the ISTE Standards!

Each level in this book connects you to the ISTE Standards for educators and students, as these standards are designed to empower student voice and ensure that learning is a student-driven process. They also serve as a road map for helping educators become empowered learners.

In this level, we learned how the power of play can increase learner engagement. We explored the concepts of game-based learning and gamification, and established a framework for game-based learning through the #PowerUpClassroom 4 C's of GBL:

> ➤ **Choose:** Learners experience choice in process and product

> ➤ **Clarify:** Learners reflect on their progress in an iterative growth process

> ➤ **Connect:** Learners build relationships through common progress, skills, interest, and goals

> ➤ **Celebrate:** Learners have opportunities to celebrate both process and mastery of learning

Level 1 aligns to the following ISTE Standards:

ISTE STANDARDS FOR EDUCATORS
Standard 5: Designer

Educators design authentic, learner-driven activities and environments that recognize and accommodate learner variability.

➤ **5b.** Design authentic learning activities that align with content-area standards, and use digital tools and resources to maximize active, deep learning.

➤ **5c.** Explore and apply instructional design principles to create innovative, digital learning environments that engage and support learning.

Congratulations! You completed Level 1 of #PowerUpClassroom.

START

Define **#PowerUp Classroom Theory of Improvement for Education**.

Identify & explore the **#PowerUp Classroom 4 C's of GBL**.

Distinguish between **Gamification** and **GBL**.

Explore the power of play.

Empower students through choice.

Assess players' sources of motivation.

Explore the **#PowerUp Classroom GBL Design Framework**.

Clarify the role of technology in game design.

Value having fun with your learners.

Create an emotionally safe space.

Determine the purpose of student game design.

Apply **#PowerUp Classroom GBL Design Framework** to student games

Assess the impact of audience.

Establish the assessment potential of GBL.

Explain how GBL offers choice & clarification.

Assess mastery using GBL & gamification.

FINISH

Identify your next step with GBL!

Explore the power of celebration.

Assess your classroom cultural readiness.

Investigate the social-emotional dynamics of GBL.

LEVEL 2

CHOOSE YOUR ADVENTURE: OPTIONS, CHOICE, AND OWNERSHIP

How does choice impact instruction?

By the end of this level, you will be able to:

★ Empower and engage students through instructional choice
★ Create an emotionally safe space for exploration and failure
★ Consider the impact of audience, purpose, design, and relationships
★ Have more fun with your learners

I magine that you are sitting at an Italian restaurant where you are presented with one of three menus:

> The first has a laundry list of pizza toppings, pastas, and salads.

> The next one has several house specials as well as the signature pizza.

> The last one simply describes the pasta of the day.

Which one catches your eye? Why?

Choice, whether it's open or controlled, has a direct impact on how much we buy into any situation. While the extravagant and option-filled menu leaves room for each of us to design our dream meal, is it the best option for the restaurant owner, who has to be ready to serve all the unique meals? What if those choices leave the customer feeling overwhelmed or, worse, uninterested in ordering at all?

On the other hand, someone may look at the abbreviated menus and wonder how they can customize the house specials. Others might see the limited choice as a welcome approach to the meal and totally vibe with the simplicity of the experience.

♥ POWER UP

BUILD AUTHENTIC COLLABORATION

Instead of expecting children to master every content piece, help them collaborate to divide and conquer. By sharing the tasks, your students take ownership of their part in a more personal way. Investment increases and so does the quality of the work.

Likewise, even though we enjoy choice and options as consumers, we don't always carry that same level of customization into the classroom as educators.

We want students to take risks and learn through failure without fear of major setbacks. The pure joy of play creates limitless options for exploration. But, like the lengthy menu, limitless options can also turn into a burden that eventually undoes itself. K. R. Ginsburg explains the role of play in education as follows:

> *Play is integral to the academic environment. It ensures that the school setting attends to the social and emotional development of children as well as their cognitive development.... Play and unscheduled time that allow for peer interactions are important components of social-emotional learning (2007).*

It's not realistic to think that any of us will successfully complete every task we set out to achieve. A better question to consider: **Are you enjoying the process?**

MEET THE GAME MASTER

ANN BRUCKER, GAME DEVELOPER, BREAKOUT EDU

A LITTLE STRUGGLE IS WORTH IT

A few years ago, Ann Brucker attended the ISTE Conference & Expo in Denver, Colorado, and noticed how taken the attendees were by the Breakout EDU bus that parked in front of the convention center. Attendees waited their turn to enter a yellow school bus that was outfitted like a mini escape room. Players had to collaborate to solve challenges and unlock boxes that contained more codes until the problem was solved. It was different, intriguing, and memorable.

She wasn't able to get in there and experience a Breakout game firsthand that trip, but she persisted, eventually getting her hands on a Breakout EDU kit, which included a box, locks, access to a Breakout game, and permission to play. She was ready to re-create the magic of the Breakout EDU bus in her classroom!

She took the kit into her classroom of fourth graders, and without really knowing what to expect or much about the clues and game itself, she had them play the game. She wasn't able to feed them information or help them solve the puzzles since she didn't know the answers to the riddles and challenges. As she observed these kids and felt the energy in the air, she heard lots of "what-ifs." She began to hear a mantra running in her head: "Try something different. Try something different. Try something different."

As she watched her students struggle, fail, and eventually succeed, she thought: "This would be a perfect way to train teachers who have to be at my PD." So she decided to write a Breakout EDU game for them.

She introduced the Breakout EDU box and her original game to the teachers, and they dove in. Similar to her fourth graders, they started struggling, wondering, and getting a little stuck. This time, she went over and helped them by whispering a hint or providing a clue as they came up against a challenge. She knew the game inside and out, and wanted to simply help. Ann describes what happened next:

> *I had lightning strike me on the head and thought, "I've been swooping in for eighteen years and hoping that by giving my students an answer or a clue, they would get it. But they didn't. As a teacher, I've been doing this wrong for eighteen years. Shut up and let them struggle!!"*

As it turns out, Ann's passion for educational games and Breakout EDU specifically landed her a job with the Breakout EDU team as a game developer. Her discoveries throughout the last few years have changed the way she interacts with all the players she supports.

The powerful experience of standing by and allowing learners to struggle not only empowers them, but serves as a reminder to us that we can detach from the expertise and still be impactful, amazing educators.

According to Ann, "we're trying to right this great wrong. For too long, we've taught our students learned helplessness. Things like Breakout EDU, engineering, and design thinking exist to let kids take back their learning and own how (and how well) they learn."

Her sage wisdom is wrapped up in this simple thought:

> *Listen. Listen to the quiet, shy kids who never want to say anything. They are so smart! Everyone has a chance to learn when you step back and let them.*

To discover a few of Ann's favorite free digital Breakout EDU games, you will first need to create a Breakout EDU account (**platform.breakoutedu.com/ login**). Here are a few games you may enjoy:

Are You Ready,
Player One?

Zombie
Breakout

Helping learners explore emotions and express them in healthy ways is an important instructional goal. As Harry O'Malley details in his Edutopia article, creating authentic moments of play breaks the learning into emotional chunks that deepen the relationship between learners and content. Students remember content more deeply because they are not only learning the facts but associating an emotion to these facts as well. If you can get your students to laugh, yell, or feel a tinge of stress related to an academic game, we guarantee they are more likely to remember the experience in a totally different way.

As you think about your why and strategically build more choice into your instruction, here are a few critical elements to consider:

> **Determine your audience.** Define who will play and how familiar the players are with the content.

> **Determine your purpose.** Figure out if the game/lesson will introduce, explore, or review concepts.

> **Determine your design.** Decide how your game/lesson will engage your audience (Will it lure the audience into the learning right away? Will it provide opportunities

for choice and failure? Will the player have a chance to achieve mastery?).

> **Determine the types of relationships.** Establish how/if players will work together and whether you will provide an "opt out" or "opt in" choice.

You've just read about the different ways in which choice plays a role in your game-based learning design. Now, take a moment to record and share your thoughts!

 # YOUR CHALLENGE

Choose a challenge from below to share either on Twitter or here in this book. Or better yet, choose to do both!

> What's the sweet spot in between "too much" or "not enough" choice in your game design?

> How can you integrate choice and still instruct and assess according to a larger instructional plan?

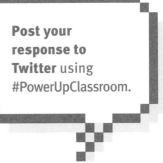

Post your response to Twitter using #PowerUpClassroom.

ISTE STANDARDS CONNECTION
Let's Connect Your Learning to the ISTE Standards!

In this level, we learned about choice and the impact it can have on the empowerment and engagement of students. We learned that incorporating choice through game-based learning can also create an emotionally safe space for students to take risks and learn through failure without fear of major setbacks.

Level 2 aligns to the following ISTE Standards:

ISTE STANDARDS FOR EDUCATORS
Standard 6: Facilitator

Educators facilitate learning with technology to support student achievement of the ISTE Standards for Students.

> **6a.** Foster a culture where students take ownership of their learning goals and outcomes in both independent and group settings.

ISTE STANDARDS FOR STUDENTS
Standard 1: Empowered Learner

Students leverage technology to take an active role in choosing, achieving, and demonstrating competency in their learning goals, informed by the learning sciences.

> **1a.** Students articulate and set personal learning goals, develop strategies leveraging technology to achieve them, and reflect on the learning process itself to improve learning outcomes.

Congratulations! You completed Level 2 of #PowerUpClassroom.

START

Define **#PowerUp Classroom Theory of Improvement** for Education.

Identify & explore the **#PowerUp Classroom 4 C's of GBL**.

Distinguish between **Gamification** and **GBL**.

Explore the power of play.

Empower students through choice.

Assess players' sources of motivation.

Explore the **#PowerUp Classroom GBL Design Framework**.

Clarify the role of technology in game design.

Value having fun with your learners.

Create an emotionally safe space.

Determine the purpose of student game design.

Apply **#PowerUp Classroom GBL Design Framework** to student games

Assess the impact of audience.

Establish the assessment potential of GBL.

Explain how GBL offers choice & clarification.

Assess mastery using GBL & gamification.

FINISH

Identify your next step with GBL!

Explore the power of celebration.

Assess your classroom cultural readiness.

Investigate the social-emotional dynamics of GBL.

LEVEL 3

ON YOUR MARK:
STRUCTURE, DESIGN, AND PURPOSE

What goes into designing meaningful and impactful instructional games?

By the end of this level, you will be able to:

★ Clarify the role that technology plays in both game design and player motivation
★ Identify the elements of the #PowerUpClassroom GBL Design Framework
★ Consider the impact of content, delivery, and assessment on game design
★ Compare your players' intrinsic and extrinsic motivators

T eam dynamics are tricky things. Some teams are highly productive, building off the strengths of each team member, and others are highly dysfunctional, struggling to work as a cohesive unit. Being a successful team member means that you need to be both a leader and a follower—often simultaneously. Ideally, you join a team because you want to explore a passion, and you genuinely care about the game or project. But hold up! Have you spent time with a group of passionate professionals lately? That can be wildly wonderful and overwhelming at the same time.

Let's think about your students. As the instructor, you are constantly weaving and remixing topics and lessons. Sometimes, technology plays a critical role in the project; other times, technology doesn't belong anywhere near the lesson.

So, determining the role of technology in your game design matters, and we have to set realistic expectations before we bring our ideas to our learners. But where do we start? Understanding the ultimate content, process, objective, and purpose of your game design is the first step in this planning process.

Let's dive into our #PowerUpClassroom GBL Design Framework (**Figure 3.1**). As we work through this, take the time to consider what areas of this framework you already have in place and what you can spend more time developing.

Oftentimes, our energy is best spent designing and building the lesson itself. The heavier lift at the beginning makes the latter stages smoother. Creating moments of learning that engage and entice learners to dive into content is the ultimate goal of any innovative educator. But what's the secret to motivating your learners? Motivation is tricky to control, so it's important to purposefully build opportunities for players to own and drive their learning.

Objective	instructional focus, standard(s), and hard skill(s) that the player will master through gameplay
Design	setting, tools, and action steps that the players will take throughout the game
Challenge	the purpose of gameplay itself
Assessment	process and elements that measure content mastery
Next Steps	extension of learning that motivates players to continue gameplay

Figure 3.1. #PowerUpClassroom GBL Design Framework

We can't always pinpoint exactly what motivates us to complete certain tasks. Sometimes, fear of "getting in trouble" at work is motivation for getting out of bed in the morning. Other times, that fear may not be enough, but considering that students depend on you to show up and teach them may be the factor that pushes us to start our day. Either way, motivation is incredibly personal and may be difficult to externally track.

Gameplay not only increases learner engagement but motivates certain learner behaviors, like persistence, inquiry, and mastery. Many social scientists believe that **extrinsic motivators** (such as money, fame, grades, praise, badges, and points) serve as only temporary rewards that will not sustain over time. **Intrinsic motivators** (like hunger for learning, self-worth, joy, intellectual growth, and curiosity) are considered more "pure," and are valued over a lifetime.

However, there is little clarity around whether external or intrinsic motivators exist independent of each other. Game-based learning incorporates extrinsic motivators like game mechanics but eventually leads to intrinsically motivated players. How will technology play a part in this entire process?

MEET THE GAME MASTER

JAMES SANDERS, FOUNDER OF BREAKOUT EDU

UNLOCKING STUDENT ENGAGEMENT

Several years ago, James was at a conference with a group of teachers and students, and the suggestion came up to go to an escape room. The teachers were surprised to see how actively engaged the students were in problem-solving—a level of engagement they had never witnessed in a traditional classroom. James began to question: How do you bring the power of an escape room into the classroom?

> *How do you bring the power of an escape room into the classroom?*

The concept is simple: There is a locked box, and students have to solve multiple challenges to unlock the box. While the concept is simple, the possibilities are endless. The lock represents the need to be right but the permission to be wrong in the process. There is no negative reaction when students input an incorrect code into a lock; they simply push forward until they get it right. This is very different from the traditional learning experience of hearing "you're wrong" and is a process that promotes perseverance in problem-solving.

If you think of the types of problems our learners are going to grow up with and have to solve and the skills they will need to solve them, from complex thinking, to working in a group, to collaborating with diverse peers, how are we empowering them to persevere through roadblocks? The major problems of today (climate change, gun control, curing cancer) are essentially locked boxes that our students will need to open.

> *The major problems of today (climate change, gun control, curing cancer) are essentially locked boxes that our students will need to open.*

NO TECH, LOW TECH, HIGH TECH

While Breakout EDU was initially designed as a game played with a physical box, it has evolved into a concept that can strategically leverage technology integration. Aside from the wide variety of both physical and digital games provided at BreakoutEDU.com, there is also a growing community of educators designing and sharing games for free. James shared that the most powerful games leverage a combination of both physical locks/challenges and digital integration, requiring students to find the necessary tools to solve a problem or challenge.

♥ POWER UP

PLAY THE GAME

The most logical entry point for someone new to Breakout EDU is to find an opportunity to play the game yourself with your colleagues. You can then debrief and explore ideas on how this might work to provide engaging learning experiences in your classroom.

Recently, Breakout EDU launched student accounts, allowing teachers to add students to their classes and assign games. One of the most powerful aspects of this new platform is that students can now design games themselves, applying their learning through game design. The teacher can then approve the games and add them to the classroom library to be played by other students in the class. (You will learn more about the shift in learning ownership through student-designed games in the next level!)

Access Breakout EDU resources at **BreakoutEDU. com**, and explore how breakouts can be applied to specific standards that fit into your curriculum at **breakoutedu.com/learning** or by scanning the QR code.

 POWER UP

MUSIC AND SOUND MAKE A DIFFERENCE!

If you want to really shake up the vibe of your learning space, integrate music and sound bites that add to the overall experience. Tone and rhythm affect workflow, and at times, the lyrics actually help to communicate expectations and objectives. See what sounds you can find, and when you find them, press "Play"!

POWER UP

MANAGE YOUR GAME SPACE

Designing a classroom space that supports game-based learning starts with clear norms that are truly internalized by all players. Start off your instruction by outlining expectations and practicing how to move and communicate in a collaborative gaming environment. You will gain so much by going slow first to eventually go fast.

YOUR CHALLENGE

Now that you've explored the content, process, objective, and purpose of your game design, take a few moments to record your thoughts and even share them! Choose a challenge from below to share either on Twitter, here in this book, or both!

➤ Based on the resources and devices you have available, how dependent on technology will you be in designing and playing games?

➤ Will you depend more on intrinsic or extrinsic motivation in your game design?

_____

_____

_____

_____

_____

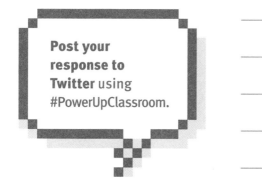

Post your response to Twitter using #PowerUpClassroom.

ISTE STANDARDS CONNECTION

Let's Connect Your Learning to the ISTE Standards!

In this level, you learned about the role technology plays in both game design and player motivation. We also identified the different elements of the #PowerUpClassroom GBL Design Framework. We then reflected on this framework through reflective questions on content, delivery, and assessment. Lastly, we looked at the impact of extrinsic and intrinsic motivation in gameplay.

Level 3 aligns to the following ISTE Standards:

 ## ISTE STANDARDS FOR EDUCATORS
Standard 5: Designer

Educators design authentic, learner-driven activities and environments that recognize and accommodate learner variability.

Indicators:

➤ **5a.** Use technology to create, adapt, and personalize learning experiences that foster independent learning and accommodate learner differences and needs.

➤ **5b.** Design authentic learning activities that align with content-area standards, and use digital tools and resources to maximize active, deep learning.

➤ **5c.** Explore and apply instructional design principles to create innovative digital-learning environments that engage and support learning.

Congratulations! You completed Level 3 of #PowerUpClassroom.

START

Define **#PowerUp Classroom Theory of Improvement** for Education.

Identify & explore the **#PowerUp Classroom 4 C's of GBL.**

Distinguish between **Gamification** and **GBL.**

Explore the power of play.

Empower students through choice.

Assess players' sources of motivation.

Explore the **#PowerUp Classroom GBL Design Framework.**

Clarify the role of technology in game design.

Value having fun with your learners.

Create an emotionally safe space.

Determine the purpose of student game design.

Apply **#PowerUp Classroom GBL Design Framework** to student games

Assess the impact of audience.

Establish the assessment potential of GBL.

Explain how GBL offers choice & clarification.

Assess mastery using GBL & gamification.

FINISH

Identify your next step with GBL!

Explore the power of celebration.

Assess your classroom cultural readiness.

Investigate the social-emotional dynamics of GBL.

LEVEL 4

THEIR TURN: STUDENTS AS GAME MASTERS

How can we empower students to grow as learners while designing games?

By the end of this level, you will be able to:

★ Formulate a clear purpose for student game design
★ Apply the #PowerUpClassroom GBL Design Framework to student game designers
★ Assess the impact of audience in game design

In the previous levels, we explored the power of shifting your role from content expert to designer of games in a way that empowers students to take increased ownership of their learning. However, the teacher is not the only potential designer and Game Master in the room. As we seek to empower students as agents of their own learning, we can step aside to allow them to become game designers while providing them with both the space and the structure that set them up for success. Step aside and watch your students rise to the occasion.

In *Culturally Responsive Teaching and the Brain*, Zaretta Hammond describes the crucial role trust plays in developing student agency:

> *Our ultimate goal is to position dependent learners so that they will take the intellectual risk and stretch into their zone of proximal development (ZPD). That's the point of rapport— building trust is designed to help dependent learners avoid the stress and anxiety that comes with feeling lost and unsupported at school.*

By empowering your students to not only consume the content they are expected to learn but also to create content to support the learning of others, you are sending a strong message of trust and ownership. Introducing student game design through a strategic process allows students to push into their ZPD both creatively and academically.

Jacob Aringo, STEAM teacher, moves his students through a low-tech to high-tech process in introducing game design. They start by creating a cardboard arcade inspired by the Caine's Arcade movement (a movement based on a documentary about a nine-year-old boy who built an entire arcade out of cardboard in his dad's used auto parts store).

Figure 4.1. Caine running his arcade. Photo: meeno (meenophoto.com), 2011.

Learn more about the movement and Caine's Arcade at
CainesArcade.com.

As Jacob's students design games for the cardboard arcade, they learn about the elements of game design. And as the course progresses, he feels himself transitioning into a digital realm, where students code their own games.

GAME DESIGN FOR STUDENTS

Are you ready to empower your students to grow as learners through game design? This section aligns the process of game design for students with our **#PowerUpClassroom GBL Design Framework**. To help you launch the process, each step includes a checklist of things to consider.

PROJECT MANAGEMENT IS NOT JUST FOR ADULTS!

Empower your students as project planners. Teach them that:

➤ Game design can be individual or collaborative, but either way, students need to know where they are going and how they are going to get there!

➤ There is a fine art of backwards planning. Have students lay out when they intend to hit significant milestones on a calendar in order to reach a final goal. And don't forget to include feedback and iteration as part of those milestones!

OBJECTIVE

Just like when we design an academic lesson or unit of study, students need to know what they are looking to share with their audience. Communicate the standard(s) that need to be addressed in the game, and work with the students to unpack what mastery of these standards looks like.

Connect these standards to a larger purpose. Ask the following questions about the students' games:

◇ Will the student demonstrate knowledge of content or academic standards through the design of the game?

◇ Will the audience that engages in the game have opportunities to learn about the content through the game?

◇ Does the game accomplish a higher purpose or deeper meaning (i.e. connecting the game to a solution to a global or local issue)?

DESIGN

As there is no "one size fits all" approach to game design, encourage your students to consider how the game will be delivered. After you have identified the elements of game design with your students, offer choice in delivery.

- Identify the elements of game design: Don't have time to build a cardboard arcade? Play a game (yes, this can even be a traditional board game!) and then discuss the game elements that made it engaging.

- Allow for choice in the medium.

  - From low-tech to no-tech to high-tech, there is no "one size fits all" answer to what platform and medium your students will prefer to design and play in.

  - Consider offering students choice between physically building a board game, creating a game with digital integrations (think of the QR codes in this book!), or coding a game that others can play.

CHALLENGE

Encourage your students to actively reflect on the purpose or overarching goal of their game as they design. One way to ensure the game has a clear purpose is to consider the audience during the design phase. Designing for an authentic audience leads to deeper engagement and purpose. To design for an authentic audience, consider the following:

- Who are your students designing for? Who will ultimately play their game?

◇ Will your students design for their peers or younger students to help them learn the content through engaging in the game?

◇ Will the game be shared with their families to foster a stronger connection between home and school?

◇ Will the game be shared with a larger local or global community in order to see the larger impacts of the students' creative work?

◇ What is the challenge that this audience will tackle through playing the game? How is this challenge deeply connected to the audience's experiences, values, or goals?

ASSESSMENT

Unlike when the teacher designs a game for students, with student-designed games, the game itself is the assessment. In the design of the game, the student needs to make sure he or she is including the target academic content.

Consider the use of rubrics as a way to help students ensure their game is meeting the targets of the lesson. New to rubric design? Check out the resources page on the PBL Works (formerly Buck Institute) site (**my.pblworks.org/resources**). It even has a "Rubric for Rubrics" resource!

THE POTENTIAL OF COLLABORATION

There are many benefits to student collaboration when they design games. Partner and team structures provide scaffolding and support throughout the learning process, giving students the opportunity to clarify their understanding and receive immediate feedback. Collaboration also provides students with competencies they will need for career success, such as complex problem-solving, critical thinking, and coordinating with others (World Economic Forum, The Future of Jobs Report 2018).

NEXT STEP

Students should engage in gathering input and active reflection following the design of a game, exploring the following questions:

- What aspects of the game worked well?

- What aspects could be adjusted in the future?

- What did I learn in designing the game?

- What did my classmates learn through playing the game?

Never underestimate the power of designing for an authentic audience. In *Leaders of Their Own Learning*, Berger, Rugen, and Woodfin (2014) describe the impact of broader audiences over students' senses of pride and accomplishment, and how this leads to implementation in both local and global communities. The authors' "Hierarchy of Audience" model **(Figure 4.2)** shows us what to consider when empowering student game design. This model suggests that student-designed games built for an authentic and global audience will lead to increased motivation and engagement.

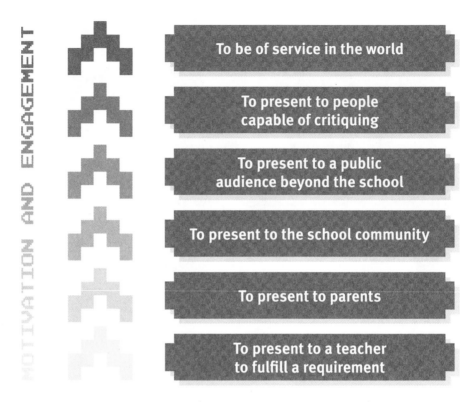

Figure 4.2. Hierarchy of Audience (Berger, Rugen, & Woodfin, 2014).

Honoring students as game designers not only allows them to engage in a strategic design process but creates a culture where students take deep ownership of their learning goals and outcomes. Let's see this in action with our Game Masters!

MEET THE GAME MASTER

CRISTINA BUSTAMANTE, STEAM COACH

WHY GAMES?

As a STEAM coach, Cristina leads her students and other teachers in innovative learning design. When asked "Why do you incorporate games into the learning experience?" she shared:

> *Games are another way to level the playing field, allowing all of our students to access and engage in content. People play games for different reasons, ranging from social aspects to individual accomplishment. If you develop games so all of these aspects are present, you will tap into the key motivations that engage players. Games are a natural outlet for differentiation. Through gaming, the learning design becomes more universal.*

As a teacher, Cristina warns that you need to become comfortable with many different things happening at once in your classroom—and it might get noisy! Be okay with productive noise and provide students with options to design independently or with partners/groups. Games might also require movement—perhaps students design physical challenges that require you to leave the classroom. Create the conditions that can make this a reality. Planning is key!

WHERE TO BEGIN?

Allow your students to actually play a game, then discuss the basics of game design:

> What do games entail?
> What makes a game fun?
> What elements need to be included so people will want to play the game?
> What is the goal or end result of the game?
> What will players get out of the game and how will they "win"?

PHYSICAL OR DIGITAL . . . OR BOTH?

As we shared in the previous level, powerful game design can take the form of no tech, low tech, or high tech. When Cristina's students design physical games, she connects to their existing knowledge of gameplay by bringing in old board games and tossing all of the pieces in a bucket. Students then engage in collaborative design with the materials they have been given and create new materials as needed, such as the game board, to bring the goals of the game to life.

 POWER UP

BUILDING PERSEVERANCE IN PROBLEM-SOLVING

When students design games, encourage them to include roadblocks! The player shouldn't be able to move from the start to the finish of a game without encountering any challenges that potentially set them back or take them on a different path. This builds a sense of accomplishment when goals are reached and develops perseverance in problem-solving.

In terms of digital game design, Cristina and her students are fans of choose your own adventure (CYOA) games as well as digital breakouts. CYOA games can be developed by both teachers and students using Google Forms, Google Docs, and Google Slides. Have students start by engaging in a game and exploring how the technical-build aspects work, then they can start to create their own story line once they are familiar with the tool's capabilities.

 # POWER UP

AVOID COGNITIVE OVERLOAD

If the students are new to the tool or to game design in general, start with review content! Don't introduce new content alongside a new tool or strategy as this will lead to cognitive overload for students. You can then transition towards game design as a way for students to tackle new content.

Want to explore some more? Here are a few suggestions:

> ❯ Access a step-by-step presentation of CYOA Google Forms at **bit.ly/FormsAdventure** or by scanning the QR code.
> ❯ Connect with Cristina on Twitter **@CBustamante2222**.

While Cristina supports the integration of games across STEAM subjects and other curricular areas, our next Game Masters show us how student game design can be seamlessly integrated into computer science.

MEET THE GAME MASTERS

BILL MARSLAND AND ANDREW ROTHMAN, COMPUTER SCIENCE SPECIALISTS

CS FOR CREATIVE GAME DESIGN

Our Game Masters advocate that computer science (CS) offers a platform where students can engage in meaningful challenges that bring together design, coding, and making (all key components for creative problem-solving). When it comes to designing through CS, you don't need to have all of the answers but, rather, need to be willing to partner with and learn alongside your students. Students can create any number of things with CS: animations, music, art, storytelling, and (you guessed it) games! According to Bill:

> *There is a misconception that computer science is something that is rigid—here is a program, copy my code, you're done. We now have tools that allow us to teach CS in such a creative way that we are able to give students agency and choice, creating things that are meaningful to them.*

Let's look at three examples of lesson design and pay attention to the levels of student engagement:

1. The student writes an essay. The teacher then reads it, grades it, and returns it (low impact).

2. The student designs a slide-deck presentation and presents it to a passive audience, receiving minimal feedback (medium impact).

3. The student designs an interactive game that peers or community members play to deepen their learning on the topic (high impact).

Andrew's Tip: Incorporate interactivity to move from passive to active engagement. When students are designing projects to share, consider how CS can be leveraged to increase the level of interactivity.

As you can see, the deeper the level of interactivity, the deeper the impact you have on student engagement. Consider how you might incorporate what we learned from the Hierarchy of Audience model as aligned with increased interactivity for designing high-impact learning experiences.

CS FOR EQUITY AND INCLUSIVITY

The field of CS enhances our ability to build an inclusive culture around technology. As part of the Computer Science team in San Francisco Unified School District and alongside their fearless leader Bryan Twarek (**@BTwarek**), much of Andrew and Bill's efforts have focused on challenging the stereotypes and identity assumptions of who a "gamer" or a "coder" is. With CS, they strive to create opportunities that allow girls and underrepresented groups to see themselves as designers, adapting pedagogy and emphasizing connections that make CS accessible.

How do Bill, Andrew, and the #CSinSF team design for equity and inclusivity?

> They intentionally use and promote videos, images, and articles about people in CS careers (including gaming) across a spectrum of race, ethnicity, gender identity/expression, and orientation in order to amplify the voices of computer scientists who challenge the traditional representation of those in the field.

> They use collaborative strategies (such as pair programming) to foster a sense of community and teamwork, and remove the sense of competition that historically existed in CS.

> They write curriculum that has open-ended assignments so that students can bring their own identity and interests into the project instead of having to recreate someone else's project, which may not reflect the students' identity and interests in the same way.

In their experience, games are naturally engaging for students. CS empowers students to design and create games that are meaningful and relevant regardless of student gender, background, and ethnicity. It allows students to design in a way that transcends the classroom, creating and easily sharing with a wide and authentic audience. According to Bill:

Just like technology integration, computer science should not be an extra, a reward, a bonus. There is so much potential for CS to be ingrained, intertwined, and woven into the curriculum. It's not, "Yay Robots!" but, rather, "How can these robots support our learning?" It shouldn't be reserved for certain students, fun Fridays, and early finishers, but should be an opportunity for each and every student.

RECOMMENDED RESOURCES TO GET STARTED

> ScratchJr (**ScratchJr.org**): a resource that allows K–2 students to design
> Scratch (**scratch.mit.edu**): a design resource for Grades 3–5
> Scratch tutorials (**scratch.mit.edu/ideas**)
> Code.org's App Lab (**bit.ly/startAppLab**): a design resource for middle school students
> Code.org's CS Discoveries, Unit 3 (**bit.ly/CSdiscoveries3**): game and animation design for middle school students

All of these resources and more can be found on the San Francisco Unified School District computer science website (**CSinSF.org**). And you can see more CS in action on Twitter at **#CSinSF**, and by connecting with Bill and Andrew: **@BillMarsland** and **@RothmanCS**.

Now that we have explored the power of inviting students to design games and some strategies for launching that process, it's *your* turn!

 # YOUR CHALLENGE

Choose a challenge from below to share either on Twitter or here in this book. Or better yet, choose to do both!

> Ask your students what makes games fun and capture their responses to share!

> Think of an upcoming lesson or unit that students might design games for. Share what this unit is and why you chose it!

Post your
response to
Twitter using
#PowerUpClassroom.

ISTE STANDARDS CONNECTION
Let's Connect Your Learning to the ISTE Standards!

In this level, we learned how to empower students as agents and owners of their learning experience by becoming game designers themselves, and we assessed the impact of audience in student game design.

Level 4 aligns to the following ISTE Standards:

ISTE STANDARDS FOR EDUCATORS
Standard 6: Facilitator

Educators facilitate learning with technology to support student achievement of the ISTE Standards for Students.

> **6a.** Foster a culture where students take ownership of their learning goals and outcomes in both independent and group settings.

> **6c.** Create learning opportunities that challenge students to use a design process and computational thinking to innovate and solve problems.

ISTE STANDARDS FOR STUDENTS

Standard 6: Creative Communicator

Students communicate clearly and express themselves creatively for a variety of purposes using the platforms, tools, styles, formats, and digital media appropriate to their goals.

Indicators:

> **6a.** Students choose the appropriate platforms and tools for meeting the desired objectives of their creation or communication.

> **6d.** Students publish or present content that customizes the message and medium for their intended audiences.

Congratulations! You completed Level 4 of #PowerUpClassroom.

START

Define **#PowerUp Classroom Theory of Improvement for Education**.

Identify & explore the **#PowerUp Classroom 4 C's of GBL**.

Distinguish between **Gamification** and **GBL**.

Explore the power of play.

Empower students through choice.

Assess players' sources of motivation.

Explore the **#PowerUp Classroom GBL Design Framework**.

Clarify the role of technology in game design.

Value having fun with your learners.

Create an emotionally safe space.

Determine the purpose of student game design.

Apply **#PowerUp Classroom GBL Design Framework** to student games

Assess the impact of audience.

Establish the assessment potential of GBL.

Explain how GBL offers choice & clarification.

Assess mastery using GBL & gamification.

FINISH

Identify your next step with GBL!

Explore the power of celebration.

Assess your classroom cultural readiness.

Investigate the social-emotional dynamics of GBL.

LEVEL 5

WHO'S WINNING? POWER UP YOUR ASSESSMENT AND FEEDBACK

How do we leverage game-based learning as a powerful assessment tool?

By the end of this level, you will be able to:

★ Distinguish between the formative and summative assessment potential of GBL
★ Explain how GBL offers the ability to choose and clarify learning
★ Clarify distinct ways to assess mastery using GBL and gamification
★ Explore high-tech GBL solutions for assessment

Grades. Rubrics. Tests. We typically use these assessment tools with our learners at the end of the lesson, unit, or project. But how might the summative assessment results shift if we gave learners formative feedback and permission to start fresh at any point along the learning journey?

GBL gives us an opportunity to be less focused on controlling the assessment and more focused on supporting our learners as they experience feedback in real time. How often do we incorporate feedback loops with our learners that allow them to see their progress and revise their path? If you had no clue how you were progressing in a game and what you needed to do to move to the next level, would you still play? Of course not!

By inviting our students to move through content at their own pace and choose the method of learning that works best for them, we are increasing the likelihood that they will retain the information and feel more invested in the learning process. Individualized instruction theory suggests that we focus more on *when* the content is learned rather then *how*. An article titled "Personalization vs. Differentiated vs. Individualized Learning" by Dale Basye (2018) describes individualized instruction as follows:

> *This approach serves students who may need to review previously covered material, students who don't want to waste time covering information they've already mastered, or students who need to proceed through the curriculum more slowly or immerse themselves in a certain topic or principle to really "get" it.*

Empowering students while they are learning helps them reach a point of clarity around the instructional what and how. Likewise, by creating failure-forward moments with chances to "do over," we remove the stifling stigma we feel when we see those results at the end (via grades, tests, and rubrics).

In a game-based learning environment, failure is just as much a part of the learning process as success. In fact, failure is a part of the entire culture. Granting permission to play and persist with the belief that every learner can and will eventually reach mastery is a complete shift from traditional classroom beliefs of bell curves and averages. We each have the opportunity to play the role of game designer and coach—a far more engaging and impactful place to instruct from.

> "Failure is instructive. The person who really thinks learns quite as much from his failures as from his successes."
> —John Dewey

While failure and persistence help players explore their growth, there are other game mechanics that act as powerful assessment tools and potential motivators as well. If your first chance was your only chance to master a game, you would never progress to mastery! How often is our first chance our only chance in learning life lessons? Hopefully not often.

MEET THE GAME MASTER

LINDSEY BLASS, PASSIONATE EDUCATOR

RETHINKING ASSESSMENT

When Lindsey started teaching, she viewed assessment as an event. She often found herself making statements such as, "Get a good night's sleep tonight, students. Tomorrow is our assessment!"

As her teaching career progressed, she discovered that assessment was an integral part of the learning process, as opposed to an event that takes place following the learning. She began to enjoy using data to see her learners' progress in their mastery of skills as they engaged in learning. The only problem was that students weren't enjoying the assessment as much as she was. Exit tickets, quick writes, and quick checks—these tools all provided Lindsey with valuable data as she went home to see where her students were and plan for the next day, but they lacked the interactivity and immediate feedback that would engage her students in the process.

When Lindsey discovered powerful game-based assessment tools, *her* entire game changed:

> *I introduced my students to digital, formative assessment tools that were also* fun! *Not only was I able to gather and share real-time data on my students' progress and performance through the use of game-based assessment tools [but] my students were so deeply engaged in the games that they would arrive at class begging for us to play!*

"Zebras! Where are the zebras?!" Lindsey's learners will yell as they make their way across the room to find their team. When was the last time (if ever) that your students came to class with as much enthusiasm for an assessment?

Lindsey's top pick for game-based collaborative assessment: Quizlet Live. Her reason for loving this tool? Students *need* each other to be successful as they work collaboratively on matching up key terms.

No student has all of the answers on their screen, so they have to engage in actual dialogue about what the right answer might be (academic discourse for the *win*). In the data, the teacher can see commonly missed terms and use this to inform their instruction. The teacher can also shuffle teams, to allow the students to take what they learned working with one group and teach it to their next team. Learn more about this tool at **Quizlet.com** or by scanning the QR code.

 POWER UP

IT'S NOT ABOUT THE TECH

While digital formative assessment tools are powerful for both engagement and feedback, if you are introducing a new tool every day, you are doing it wrong. To start, strategically choose one or two digital assessment tools to bring into your instruction and work these in on a semiregular basis (about one to three times per week).

When it comes to game-based individual assessment, Lindsey's top pick is Quizizz (**quizizz.com**). Quizizz provides memes that instantly indicate if a student answered correctly or incorrectly. It also provides opportunities for a student to play a game as many times as he or she needs to achieve mastery (multiple lives, if you will), including the ability to turn the timer off for individualized pacing and the ability to turn the leaderboard off so a student can just compete against his or her personal best. (A bonus tip from Lindsey: have your students make their own correct/incorrect memes in Google Slides and import these into Quizizz, so they see themselves in the game!)

Access resources from Lindsey's various presentations at her website, **LindseyBlass.com**.

Making mastery more visible shifts the emphasis from product to process. Two powerful tools for visually acknowledging the learning are badges and microcredentials. When rewarded incrementally, players see their growth and accomplishments in real time. But what's the difference between these two tools? The reality is that badges and micro-credentials often work hand-in-hand.

To unpack it further, the badges are images that represent mastery with a name and a design. There are two types: closed and open badges. Closed badges are simply image files; open badges are images that, when clicked, link to data that further explains what the earner did to get that badge and identifies the mastered skill itself. This powerful metadata can include the date that it was earned, the name of the earner, and even a link to the evidence submitted.

When open badges are a part of a larger badge-earning system, they can stand alone or stack with other open badges. Together, the internal metadata (via blockchain technology) combined with the visual badges are known as microcredentials. The data points within the microcredentials document nano-learning chunks that communicate areas of interest and methods of learning in a really personalized way.

These data points invite players to track their learning, share it, revisit it from time to time, and use it to inform next steps and new areas to explore. Similarly, points and leaderboards help players see their personal progress as it compares to others or to their own learning patterns. Educators who choose to bring badging into their classroom often start by shifting a certain content area or unit of study. By starting small, students are able to see the benefits of evidence-based learning in real time—how it feels to acknowledge the learning as it happens—and all while persisting through failure and success. Therein lies a powerful instructional solution.

♥ POWER UP

REAL-TIME FEEDBACK FTW (FOR THE WIN!)

Just because you are the teacher doesn't mean you have to be the traditional assessor. Leverage technology and game design to be the assessment tool so that you can help players process the feedback rather than tirelessly do the grading. You have so much more to offer than red ink!

MEET THE GAME MASTER

GREGG EILERS, PROJECT COORDINATOR, EDUCATIONAL TECHNOLOGY, SCOE

FLIPPING PD

In 2016, Gregg and his team at the Stanislaus County Office of Education (SCOE) in Modesto, California, decided to flip professional learning on its head and integrate a digital badging platform for educators to explore and assess their own learning. They wondered: What are ways we can support [educators] to grow and be proficient in certain areas as opposed to sit-and-get, one-size-fits-all PD?

The SCOE Badge Project allows learners both inside and outside the county to choose the areas of digital learning that they are interested in exploring and then move at their own pace—it's all ultra-personalized. And rather than waiting for the end of a unit to provide feedback, badges are earned incrementally at three levels:

> **Level 1**: just learn and see what the topic is and why it exists
> **Level 2**: create something that you can use in your classroom or with other staff
> **Level 3**: implement the resource and reflect on how the topic/ resource shifts learning

The empowerment of ongoing formative feedback helps SCOE badge earners manage their own progress. Learners own the learning process from the beginning through embedded choice in the badge pathways. And as more educators participate in the program, they shift from earning to designing student badging systems for assessment and celebration in their own communities.

The widespread engagement with this platform is impressive, with certain districts requiring educators to earn SCOE badges as part of their adopted professional learning program. Some rewards even include community-solicited prizes and points shown on a leaderboard. Even better, as educators experience gamified digital learning and assessment in really personal ways, the strategy is ultimately making its way into classrooms for the benefit of all their students too. According to Gregg:

> *It's brought in people who wouldn't have normally learned this way. Students are [now] creating criteria for what students need to know because educators are taking the model with adult learners and applying it in their classrooms.*

Want to learn more about the SCOE Badge Project? Visit the project website (**bit.ly/SCOEbadgeproject**), scan the QR code, or connect with Gregg on Twitter (**@greggeilers**).

After considering the overall positive impact of failure in the learning process and the potential instructional wins of games as the assessment, it's your turn to reflect and share!

YOUR CHALLENGE

Choose a challenge from below to share either on Twitter or here in this book. Or better yet, choose to do both!

> What aspects of games do you see as useful ways to assess?

> How do you appreciate getting feedback while playing games? Can you transfer any of these strategies into the games you design for your learners? How?

Post your response to Twitter using #PowerUpClassroom.

ISTE STANDARDS CONNECTION

Let's Connect Your Learning to the ISTE Standards!

In this level, we learned how to leverage game-based learning as a powerful assessment tool. We saw how GBL offers learners a chance to choose what they learn and how they learn it with certain tools, like badges and microcredentials. Finally, we looked at high-tech GBL solutions for assessment.

Level 5 aligns to the following ISTE Standards:

ISTE STANDARDS FOR EDUCATORS
Standard 7: Analyst

Educators understand and use data to drive their instruction, and support students in achieving their learning goals.

Indicators:

> **7a.** Provide alternative ways for students to demonstrate competency and reflect on their learning using technology.

> **7b.** Use technology to design and implement a variety of formative and summative assessments that accommodate learner needs, provide timely feedback to students, and inform instruction.

ISTE STANDARDS FOR STUDENTS
Standard 1: Empowered Learner

Students leverage technology to take an active role in choosing, achieving, and demonstrating competency in their learning goals, informed by the learning sciences.

Indicators:

> **1c.** Students use technology to seek feedback that informs and improves their practice and to demonstrate their learning in a variety of ways.

Congratulations! You completed Level 5 of #PowerUpClassroom.

START

Define **#PowerUp Classroom Theory of Improvement** for Education.

Identify & explore the **#PowerUp Classroom 4 C's of GBL.**

Distinguish between **Gamification** and **GBL.**

Explore the power of play.

Empower students through choice.

Assess players' sources of motivation.

Explore the **#PowerUp Classroom GBL Design Framework.**

Clarify the role of technology in game design.

Value having fun with your learners.

Create an emotionally safe space.

Determine the purpose of student game design.

Apply **#PowerUp Classroom GBL Design Framework** to student games

Assess the impact of audience.

Establish the assessment potential of GBL.

Explain how GBL offers choice & clarification.

Assess mastery using GBL & gamification.

FINISH

Identify your next step with GBL!

Explore the power of celebration.

Assess your classroom cultural readiness.

Investigate the social-emotional dynamics of GBL.

LEVEL 6

BUILD YOUR SQUAD: COMMUNITY AND CULTURE THROUGH GAMEPLAY

How can games impact classroom culture and help connect players?

By the end of this level, you will be able to:

★ Establish the emotional impact of single-player versus multiplayer GBL
★ Investigate the social dynamics of GBL
★ Assess your own classroom's cultural readiness for GBL
★ Explore the power of celebration as an instructional and cultural tool

As educators, we start each day hoping to build relationships that invigorate learning and redefine the way that we interact with our learners. Whether it's in the parking lot, cafeteria, or right inside the classroom at 7:30 a.m., we are always trying to create safe, engaging learning environments. But sometimes, games actually push students out of their comfort zone too fast.

Consider the game of Monopoly. Have you ever sat down to play a light round and an hour later, felt your insides bubbling from pure frustration? Maybe it's the excitement of winning money mixed with the disappointment of having to pay other players; perhaps it's the random chance cards that spike our emotions; or maybe it's the dance between "free parking" and going "straight to jail." Whatever the spark is, Monopoly can bring friends together and break them apart. Knowing that games might engage and alienate learners is a powerful step in figuring out the role that game-based learning has with your community of learners.

Depending on your vision for GBL delivery, one-player versus multi-player games can both affect the relationship-building process. Consider Quizlet, a digital game platform that encourages players to simply quiz themselves or their team, or to test their knowledge of the content against the content only. The player has the opportunity to both fail and succeed less publicly. If prompted, the player might report his or her progress, but the actual gameplay happens very personally.

But what happens to the social dynamics when the game becomes a multiplayer, collaborative experience? The social impact of multi-player gameplay can work for and against the design. As facilitators, we must ensure that the players are able to move through these experiences positively.

♥ POWER UP

BE ON THE LOOKOUT FOR REASONS TO CELEBRATE

As the instructional leader and head designer, remember to keep your eyes and ears open for celebration and teachable moments that lead to positive feedback. We can always be looking to share meaningful and true compliments with our learners, and in so doing, we are giving them permission to do the same. That's how culture shifts.

So let's take a moment to analyze the importance of cultural readiness in game-based learning. If instructional failure is not viewed as a productive tool of learning in your community, then public failure sets back a player's confidence and works against your goals as the game designer. No one wants to alienate a player, so acknowledging ways that game design might set players apart has to be considered.

MEET THE GAME MASTER

RYAN O'DONNELL, EDUCATOR AND GAME ENTHUSIAST

FROM GAME PADAWAN TO JEDI MASTER

Back when Ryan was a student teacher, he sat to the side watching Jack, his master teacher, run a review using a Jeopardy-style game, with index cards taped to his whiteboard. Ryan looked at the new computer in front of him (with PowerPoint running on Windows 3.1) and thought, "I can make that game look better." So he did. The functionality wasn't totally the same, but he felt like the look was far superior; and he thought that alone made it better.

He spent the next ten years making review games that "looked good." One day, he stood to the side, watching his students play his review version of Who Wants to be a Millionaire?, and he felt himself hit a rock bottom.

He saw one student playing and thirty-four students watching. "This is more about me and the game," he thought. "Most of the kids aren't even playing." He vowed in that moment to focus on student engagement and get more kids involved. He considered: What if they don't answer the questions but demonstrate the learning in a different way?

> *What if they don't answer the questions but demonstrate the learning in a different way?*

Soon, Ryan developed his game, Frazzle, which mimics The $100,000 Pyramid. Students began to run in teams to demonstrate the learning and not just answer review questions. He soon saw his role shift to be a game-show host rather than the star of the show. He saw the power of letting the students play while he sat back and watched. Then, after a round, he would reteach, congratulate the players, and celebrate the learning.

Game-based learning is built to be fun and exciting, but not everyone wants to play. You still have to recognize a learner who is not willing to participate, acknowledge her or his social-emotional state, and gently nudge in the right way.

> *We have to be a life coach, counselor, and game-show host, all at the same time. Game-based learning should be* fun. *You can't force fun. Instead, you have to be able to sell fun.*

To learn more about Ryan's game resources and presentations, visit his Creative Ed Tech website (**creativeedtech.weebly.com**) or connect with him on Twitter (**@creativeedtech**).

How can you make sure your classroom culture is ready for multiplayer gameplay? The flowchart in **Figure 6.1** shows points you should consider.

Figure 6.1

IS YOUR CLASSROOM COMMUNITY READY FOR MULTIPLAYER GAMES?

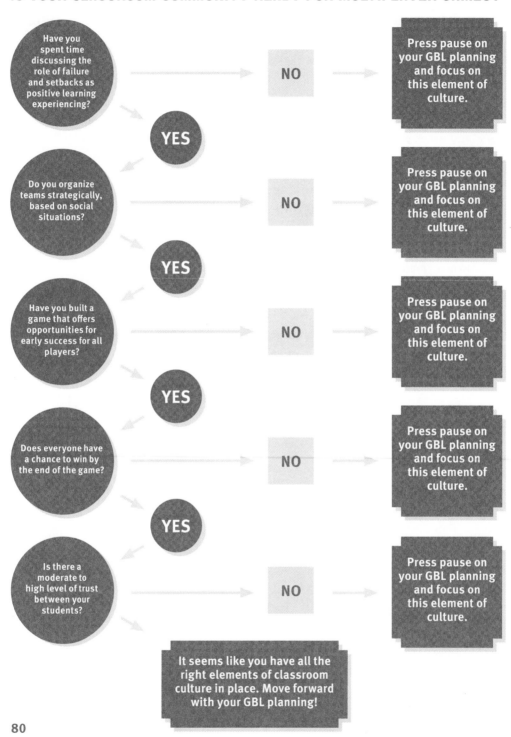

Have you spent time discussing the role of failure and setbacks as positive learning experiencing?

NO → Press pause on your GBL planning and focus on this element of culture.

YES

Do you organize teams strategically, based on social situations?

NO → Press pause on your GBL planning and focus on this element of culture.

YES

Have you built a game that offers opportunities for early success for all players?

NO → Press pause on your GBL planning and focus on this element of culture.

YES

Does everyone have a chance to win by the end of the game?

NO → Press pause on your GBL planning and focus on this element of culture.

YES

Is there a moderate to high level of trust between your students?

NO → Press pause on your GBL planning and focus on this element of culture.

It seems like you have all the right elements of classroom culture in place. Move forward with your GBL planning!

NEVER UNDERESTIMATE THE IMPACT OF A HIGH FIVE

With all the talk about rewards and prizes, just remember that kind eye contact, a knowing smile, and a high five can sometimes be exactly what celebration calls for. Getting in touch with the currency of your learners and staying open to suggestions from the students themselves continues to build a culture of shared buy-in.

If you answered no to any of these questions in **Figure 6.1**, note your starting point(s) for creating a culture that's ready for the tender, emotional impact of multiplayer gameplay.

Like we've mentioned before, celebration should be at the core of your daily interactions with you learners. Building in organic moments of celebration during and after gameplay is also a simple way to shift culture and build more positive feelings around game-based learning. Rewards, whether tangible (points, prizes, or badges) or intangible (verbal praise, extension opportunities, or increased status), are simple ways for you to shine light on players and celebrate the growth as it is taking place.

Some unintended (and awesome) outcomes of gameplay in the classroom:

> ❯ Learners having fun

> ❯ Learners being more engaged in activities and assignments

> ❯ Learners feeling more confident about content and willing to help other learners when they are stuck or lost

> Learners taking the initiative to design game-based learning experiences for each other

While we hope that the players feel the endorphin high of success on a regular basis, we can't always guarantee when that will happen or what that will look like. So taking the time to know our players, to stay in touch with the social dynamics at play from day to day, and to discover the valuable currency of each community are crucial steps to the game-design process and general culture.

MEET THE GAME MASTER

DIANE MAIN, MINECRAFT GLOBAL MENTOR

MAKE WAY FOR THE STUDENT-EXPERTS

In the fall of 2012, Diane was approached by a chemistry teacher at her school who asked her if it was okay to allow her student to build his molecular model project in Minecraft. Neither Diane nor her peer knew anything about the game but were intrigued by the student's suggestion.

This question, paired with Diane's curiosity, drove her to connect with other passionate educators and become part of the first small cohort of global Minecraft mentors. She quickly saw lots of constructivist elements in Minecraft; and the more she played inside the worlds with her students, the more she saw the collaborative and community-based power of the game.

It's not a level playing field because some kids know more. But they get in and know they have to rely on each other.

Speaking of an unlevel playing field, Diane quickly admitted that she had a lot to learn inside Minecraft, but she knew she wanted to make learning more awesome. She asked her students to choose one thing to teach her, and that morphed into opportunities for her to communicate CS terms as an unintended consequence.

> *When some of the best resources are actually crowdsourced YouTube videos made by nine- and ten-year-olds, you start to realize that you are not the holder of all the expertise anymore.*

Diane offers the following eye-opening tip:

> *Don't wait until you're an expert before you allow the students to use [Minecraft] because you'll be waiting forever. You will never know more about [Minecraft] than the kids; they're excited to help you. Don't hold back because you're not confident. Instead, commit to getting help from your learners.*

For more about Minecraft, access Minecraft's "Education Edition" resources at **education.minecraft.net** or by scannin the QR code. You can also connect with Diane on Twitter **@Dowbiggin**.

After considering the cultural readiness of GBL classrooms, it's your turn to reflect and share!

Level 6

 ☆ **YOUR CHALLENGE**

Choose a challenge from below to share either on Twitter or here in this book. Or better yet, choose to do both!

> ❯ How can you stay emotionally connected to your classroom culture and use that knowledge to responsively design games and lessons?

> ❯ How can you make more room for student-created games in your instructional design?

Post your response to Twitter using #PowerUpClassroom.

_____

_____

_____

_____

_____

_____

ISTE STANDARDS CONNECTION
Let's Connect Your Learning to the ISTE Standards!

In this level, we discovered how GBL can help connect players and how classroom culture is impacted by gameplay. We assessed our classroom's cultural readiness for GBL and spent time exploring the impact of celebration on relationships, culture, and learning.

Level 6 aligns to the following ISTE Standards:

ISTE STANDARDS FOR EDUCATORS
Standard 4: Collaborator

Educators dedicate time to collaborate with both colleagues and students to improve practice, discover, and share resources and ideas, and solve problems.

Indicators:

> **4c.** Use collaborative tools to expand students' authentic, real-world learning experiences by engaging virtually with experts, teams, and students, locally and globally.

ISTE STANDARDS FOR STUDENTS
Standard 7: Global Collaborator

Students use digital tools to broaden their perspectives and enrich their learning by collaborating with others and working effectively in teams, locally and globally.

Indicators:

> **7a.** Students use digital tools to connect with learners from a variety of backgrounds and cultures, engaging with them in ways that broaden mutual understanding and learning.

> **7b.** Students use collaborative technologies to work with others, including peers, experts, and community members, to examine issues and problems from multiple viewpoints.

Congratulations! You have completed your #PowerUpClassroom quest!

START

Define **#PowerUp Classroom Theory of Improvement for Education.**

Identify & explore the **#PowerUp Classroom 4 C's of GBL.**

Distinguish between **Gamification** and **GBL.**

Explore the power of play.

Empower students through choice.

Assess players' sources of motivation.

Explore the **#PowerUp Classroom GBL Design Framework.**

Clarify the role of technology in game design.

Value having fun with your learners.

Create an emotionally safe space.

Determine the purpose of student game design.

Apply **#PowerUp Classroom GBL Design Framework** to student games

Assess the impact of audience.

Establish the assessment potential of GBL.

Explain how GBL offers choice & clarification.

Assess mastery using GBL & gamification.

FINISH

Identify your next step with GBL!

Explore the power of celebration.

Assess your classroom cultural readiness.

Investigate the social-emotional dynamics of GBL.

LEVEL 7

PRESS START: POWER UP YOUR CLASSROOM *NOW*!

What will game-based learning look like in your classroom?

★ Review the #Power Up Classroom GBL Design Framework
★ Plan your vision for GBL
★ Connect with others around GBL and gamification

aking an idea or theory and actually putting it into action in your classroom requires time, commitment, and motivation. Hopefully, your progress through this book has brought you to a place of confidence, but just in case, here is a handy checklist to help you strategically plan your vision for game-based learning using the #PowerUpClassroom GBL Design Framework (**Figure 7.1**).

Objective	instructional focus, standard(s), and hard skill(s) that the player will master through gameplay
Design	setting, tools, and action steps that the players will take throughout the game
Challenge	the purpose of gameplay itself
Assessment	process and elements that measure content mastery
Next Steps	extension of learning that motivates players to continue gameplay

Figure 7.1. #PowerUpClassroom GBL Design Framework

Objective: Consider:

○ What is the instructional focus for the game?

○ Which standards align to your focus?

○ Which hard skills will your learners be challenged to master?

Structure: Ask yourself:

○ Will you create a fully immersive game experience (game-based learning) or will you insert game mechanics into classroom activities (gamification)?

○ What role will educational technology play in the game itself (no-tech, low-tech, or high-tech)?

Challenge: Some common challenges are:

➢ **Solve:** Players explore mysteries, embark on learning quests, answer trivia questions, and participate in strategy and logic puzzles.

➢ **Hide-and-seek:** Players travel on journeys that include themes of escape and hunt.

➢ **Build:** Players construct physical and virtual worlds, as well as participate in economies like farming and trade.

➢ **Collect:** Players gather resources to hit a winning target while factoring in qualities like time and location.

➢ **Control:** Players battle to command other players with strength, skill, and strategy to eventually overpower the other.

➢ **Survive:** Players engage in strategy puzzles with a solution that ends in life or death for the character.

Consider:

○ What is the ultimate challenge?

○ How will this be achieved?

○ How will the players interact with the content? With each other? Inside the world/game?

○ How will that interaction impact interpersonal relationships when the game is not being played?

○ Which game objective is the right fit for your focus, your learners, and your content?

Assessment: When it comes to assessment, ask yourself:

- How will you measure mastery of the content?

- Who will measure the mastery—the learner, the players, and/or the instructor?

- How will you help your learners showcase their mastery?

Next Steps: Going forward, consider:

- What will your players be encouraged to do once mastery is achieved in your game/lesson?

- Are there opportunities to "power up" the learning? What are they?

As you go forth in your learning design journey, we encourage you to revisit the #PowerUpClassroom Theory of Improvement (**Figure 7.2**).

We challenge you to:

- go forward and design learning experiences that harness the power of play,

- empower students to become active agents and owners of their learning,

- create authentic opportunities for creative problem-solving.

Figure 7.2. #PowerUpClassroom Theory of Improvement for Education

Teachers are designers who also need feedback and iteration in their design process. Keep connected with the larger Power Up Classroom community on Twitter (**#PowerUpClassroom**) and create more immediate communities by pairing up with a colleague or team on your journey! You can also use the book study guide in the appendix to engage your teams and colleagues in discussion around the potential power of play in learning.

Congratulations!

**YOUR JOURNEY TO BECOME A GAME
MASTER HAS OFFICIALLY BEGUN.**

NOW, GO POWER UP YOUR CLASSROOM!

APPENDIX A

GLOSSARY—LET'S TALK GAMES!

As you enter the world of game design, these key terms will help you engage in discussing and sharing gameplay in education.

avatar. A make-believe identity inside a virtual game or setting

badge. A visual award for achieving a level or showing mastery/competency

boss battle. The final battle at the end of a mission or quest (where a student demonstrates competency of the objectives within the quest)

digital games. Computer-based activities that weave together fun, rewards, learning, and (often) competition

end user. The person playing the game

experience points (XP). Points you earn during gameplay

Game Masters. Educators experienced in integrating gameplay into curricular design

game mechanics. Elements of gameplay (i.e., points, quests, rules, competition, badges)

gamification. The use of game mechanics (i.e., points, quests, rules, competition, badges) in nontraditional environments to make learning fun and engaging

mission. A stage within a quest that can contain course content and objectives

progress bar. A visual representation of progress toward a goal

quest. A multistep task or journey that a player or group of players completes during gameplay

reward. Points or badges awarded for completing a task

simulation. An experience designed to look and feel like something else (often used to train people and help build empathy in players)

virtual reality. A make-believe world that includes computer-generated images and sounds based on player behavior

APPENDIX B

BOOK STUDY GUIDE

Excited to get started in leveraging the power of play to increase learner engagement? Deepen your experience through collaborative dialogue with your professional learning network (PLN).

TIPS FOR RUNNING A SUCCESSFUL BOOK STUDY

> **Assemble a motivated study group** by allowing participants to voluntarily opt in or by recruiting strategically, based on common passions and varied expertise and experience.

> **Create a reading schedule** that allows for enough time to digest content but is ambitious enough that you don't lose participants through inactivity. (For this book, one level per week is a realistic amount.)

> **Create a meeting schedule** that includes live launch and closure meetings, but also use virtual communication tools such as Voxer (walkie-talkie app) or Marco Polo (video-message app) for when a concept strikes and you can't wait to share it!

> ꓩ **Provide guiding questions ahead of time** so participants can jot down notes and highlight ideas that connect back to these questions. (Lucky you—there are reflective questions included below!)

> ꓩ **Choose a discussion facilitator** to ensure equity of voices and to keep conversation student centered and solutions oriented.

> ꓩ **Share your experience** on Twitter at **#PowerUpClassroom** and tag your authors **@LindseyBlass1** and **@CateTolnai**. We would love to hear your ideas!

GUIDING QUESTIONS FOR BOOK STUDY

Introduction

In the introduction, we shared the trends we have noticed in education:

Trend 1: Learners who struggle to own and connect to their learning become disengaged.

Trend 2: Both students and teachers experience fear of failure on a regular basis.

Trend 3: Educators need support to design deeply engaging learning experiences and classroom environments where failure is celebrated as an opportunity for growth.

Trend 4: Students coming from a failure-rich classroom experience regular choice and celebration, and show much higher levels of engagement in learning.

> Which of these trends have you seen evidence of in your experience as an educator? How do you currently go about addressing these challenges?

Level 1: Beyond the Instruction Manual— Goals of the Game

What gameplay structures already exists in learning, and how can the power of play increase learner engagement?

> How do you define "student engagement"?

> What do you do to empower your learners?

> In your own words, describe the difference between gamification and game-based learning. What confusion still exists?

> Explore your "why" for embarking on this journey. What do you hope to accomplish in bringing the power of play into your learning experiences?

Level 2: Choose Your Adventure—Options, Choice, and Ownership

How does choice impact instruction?

Consider this quote when answering the questions that follow:

Choice, whether it's open or controlled, has a direct impact on how much we buy into any situation.

> ❥ What role does choice play in your classroom?

> ❥ How can you describe your experience with collaboration as it relates to investment in learning? (This can be a personal anecdote or something you have witnessed in your students.)

> ❥ What's the sweet spot in between "too much" or "not enough" choice in your game design?

> ❥ Which critical element do you consider your top priority? (audience, purpose, design, types of relationships)

> ❥ How can you integrate choice and still instruct and assess according to a larger instructional plan?

Level 3: On Your Mark—Structure, Design, and Purpose

What goes into designing meaningful and impactful instructional games?

> ❥ Based on the resources and devices you have available, how dependent on technology will you be in designing and playing games?

> ❥ Which component of the #PowerUpClassroom GBL Design Framework do you feel you already have in place? Which component will be a challenge for you to explore?

> ❥ Will you depend more on intrinsic or extrinsic motivation in your game design?

Level 4: Their Turn—Students as Game Masters

How can we empower students to grow as learners while designing games?

> What benefits do you see to student-designed games?

> What games do your students already play? How can you use these games as a catalyst for a strategic talking point around the elements of effective game design?

> What lessons or units that you teach lend themselves to student-designed games?

> How do you envision leveraging the provided #PowerUp-Classroom GBL Design Framework checklist to launch game design with your students?

> What hesitations do you have around students designing games? How can you plan to address these hesitations?

Level 5: Who's Winning? Power Up Your Assessment and Feedback

How do we leverage game-based learning as a powerful assessment tool?

> What methods of assessment do you currently use?

> Do students have multiple opportunities to work toward mastery? Are they motivated to work toward mastery?

> What role does failure play in your learning environment?

> How can you make mastery of learning more visible for your learners?

> How do you appreciate getting feedback while playing games? Can you transfer any of these strategies into the games you design for your learners?

Level 6: Build Your Squad—Community and Culture through Gameplay

How can games impact classroom culture and help connect players?

> What current collaborative norms do you have in your classroom? How can these norms be applied to game-based learning?

> What happens to social dynamics when a game is designed for single-player versus multi-player mode?

> What does celebration look like in your learning space?

> How do you stay emotionally connected to your classroom culture? How can you use that knowledge to responsively design games and lessons?

> Is your classroom community ready for multi-player games?

Level 7: Press Start—Power Up Your Classroom Now!

What will game-based learning look like in your classroom?

> What will be your biggest GBL hurdle: time, commitment, or motivation?

> Which of the defined challenge types is most intriguing to you?

> - Solve
> - Hide-and-Seek
> - Build
> - Collect
> - Control

- Survive

➤ What is one immediate strategy you can commit to implementing in order to design deeply engaging learning experiences for your students?

➤ After reading this book, which concept resonates with you and inspires you to take your next step with GBL (aka your "golden nugget")?

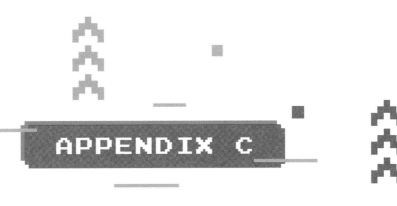

GAME DESIGN THEORIES AND FRAMEWORKS

Use these theories and frameworks as part of your game design toolkit. Refer back to them and the chapters where they are described as you continue to design and refine game-based learning experiences for your students!

#POWERUPCLASSROOM THEORY OF IMPROVEMENT

Defined in the introduction to this book, this theory describes what is possible when educators leverage game-based learning to engage and motivate learners!

Figure 0.2. #PowerUpClassroom Theory of Improvement for Education

#POWERUPCLASSROOM 4 C'S OF GAME-BASED LEARNING (GBL)

Appearing first in Level 1, the following graphic maps GBL to the 4 C's.

1. Choose: Learners experience choice in process and product

2. Clarify: Learners reflect on their progress in an iterative growth process

3. Connect: Learners build relationships through common progress, skills, interest, and goals

4. Celebrate: Learners have opportunities to celebrate both process and mastery of learning

#POWERUPCLASSROOM GBL DESIGN FRAMEWORK

The authors' framework for using game-based learning to power up classroom learning. The framework is described for educators in Level 3 and students in Level 4.

Objective	instructional focus, standard(s), and hard skill(s) that the player will master through gameplay
Design	setting, tools, and action steps that the players will take throughout the game
Challenge	the purpose of gameplay itself
Assessment	process and elements that measure content mastery
Next Steps	extension of learning that motivates players to continue gameplay

Figure 3.1. #PowerUpClassroom GBL Design Framework

REFERENCES

Basye, D. (2018). Personalized Vs. Differentiated Vs. Individualized Learning. [Blog post] Retrieved from https://www.iste.org/explore/Education-leadership/Personalized-vs.-differentiated-vs.-individualized-learning

Berger, R., Rugen, L., & Woodfin, L. (2014). *Leaders of their own learning: Transforming schools through student-engaged assessment*. New York, NY: Jossey-Bass.

Clark, D., Tanner-Smith, E., Hostetler, A., Fradkin, A., & Polikov, V. (2018). Substantial integration of typical educational games into extended curricula. *Journal of the Learning Sciences*, 27(2), 265–318. https://doi.org/10.1080/10508406.2017.1333431

Csikszentmihalyi, M. (2008). *Flow: The Psychology of Optimal Experience*. New York, NY: Harper Perennial.

Ginsburg, K. R. (2007). The importance of play in promoting healthy child development and maintaining strong parent-child bonds. *Pediatrics*, 119(1), 182–191.

Instructionaldesign.org (n.d.). Andragogy (Malcolm Knowles). Retrieved from https://www.instructionaldesign.org/theories/andragogy/

Macoun, P. (2018, June 28). Badging adventures part 4—The reflection [Blog post]. Retrieved from http://philmacoun.ca/badging-adventures-part-4-the-reflection

Schroeder, M. [TEDx Talks]. (2013, November 6). Living in beta: Molly Schroeder at TEDxBurnsvilleED [Video file]. Retrieved from https://www.youtube.com/watch?v=0nnYI3ePrY8

INDEX

★

★

★

★

LIKE WHAT YOU READ?
WE'D LOVE TO HEAR FROM YOU!

If you enjoyed this ISTE book, please consider leaving a review on Amazon or Barnes & Noble.

WANT TO CONNECT?

Mention this book on social media and follow ISTE on Twitter **@iste**, and Facebook or Instagram **@isteconnects**.

Have a burning question or suggestion for us? Email us at **books@ iste.org**.

Your feedback helps ISTE continue to bring you the best possible resources for teaching and learning in the digital age.

Thank you!